COLOMBIA

David Downing

Marshall Cavendish
Benchmark
New York

Library of Congress Cataloging-in-Publication Data

Downing, David, 1946-
    Colombia / David Downing.
        p. cm. — (Global hotspots)
    Includes index.
    Summary: "Discusses Colombia, its history, conflicts, and the reasons why it is currently in the news"—
    Provided by publisher.
    ISBN 978-0-7614-4759-7
    1. Colombia—Juvenile literature. I. Title.
    F2258.5.D68 2011
986.1—dc22
                                                        2009039775

 Produced for Macmillan Education Australia by
MONKEY PUZZLE MEDIA LTD
48 York Avenue, Hove BN3 1PJ, UK

Edited by Susie Brooks
Text and cover design by Tom Morris and James Winrow
Page layout by Tom Morris
Photo research by Susie Brooks and Lynda Lines
Maps by Martin Darlison, Encompass Graphics

Printed in the United States

Acknowledgments
The author and the publisher are grateful to the following for permission to reproduce copyright material:

Front cover photograph: Protesters near Medellín, Colombia, throw stones at riot police during an
anti-government demonstration. Courtesy of Corbis (Albeiro Lopera).

Corbis, 7 (Bettmann), 8 (Jean-Baptiste Rabouan/Hemis), 13 (Bettmann), 15 (Alain Nogues/Sygma), 18 (Reuters), 20 (Sergio
Dorantes), 24 (Patrick Chauvel), 27 (Reuters), 28 (Reuters); Getty Images, 4 (AFP), 6 (Time & Life Pictures), 10 (Time & Life
Pictures), 11 (Time & Life Pictures), 12 (Time & Life Pictures), 14 (Time & Life Pictures), 16 (AFP), 17 (AFP),
19, 21, 22, 23 (AFP), 25 (AFP), 26 (AFP); iStockphoto, 30; Reuters, 29 (John VIzcaino).

While every care has been taken to trace and acknowledge copyright, the publisher tenders their apologies for any
accidental infringement where copyright has proved untraceable. Where the attempt has been unsuccessful, the
publisher welcomes information that would redress the situation.

1 3 5 6 4 2

CONTENTS

Glossary Words

When a word is printed in **bold**, you can look up its meaning in the Glossary on page 31.

ALWAYS IN THE NEWS

Global hot spots are places that are always in the news. They are places where there has been conflict between different groups of people for years. Sometimes the conflicts have lasted for hundreds of years.

Why Do Hot Spots Happen?

There are four main reasons why hot spots happen:

1 Disputes over land, and who has the right to live on it.

2 Disagreements over religion and **culture**, where different peoples find it impossible to live happily side-by-side.

3 Arguments over how the government should be organized.

4 Conflict over resources, such as oil, gold, or diamonds.

Sometimes these disagreements spill over into violence—and into the headlines.

HOT SPOT BRIEFING

LATIN AMERICA
Colombia is one of many Latin American countries. These countries are in Central and South America. Most of them were ruled by Spain until the early 1900s, and Spanish remains their official language today.

Colombians march through the capital city of Bogotá in March 2008, in protest against continued violence in their country. They are carrying a huge Colombian flag.

Colombia

Colombia has been a hot spot since it was invaded by Spain in the early 1500s. From that time on, the country has suffered many **civil wars**. Most conflict has happened because the country's wealthy **elite** have been determined to keep their grip on power and money. This has made life very difficult for other Colombians.

The Drug Trade

Since the 1970s, Colombia has been a center of the world trade in illegal drugs. The drug traders are organized into groups known as **cartels**. They are wealthy, violent, and powerful. The influence of the drug cartels has made Colombia hard to govern.

Colombia lies in the north-west corner of South America. Its border with Panama links it to Central America, while the United States lies further north across the Caribbean Sea.

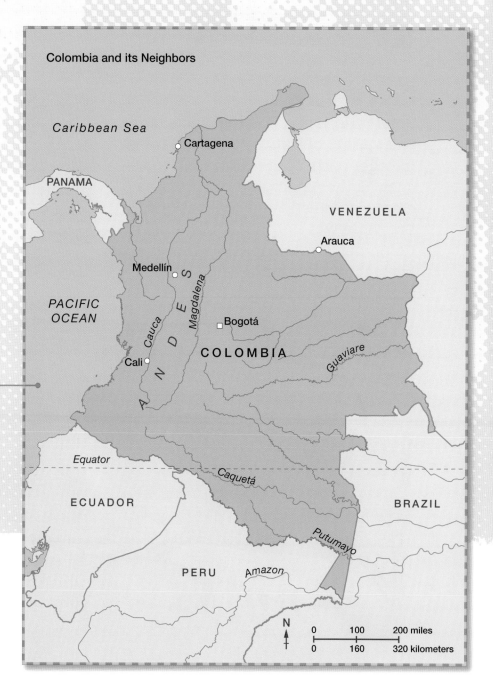

Colombia and its Neighbors

Caribbean Sea

Cartagena

PANAMA

VENEZUELA

Arauca

Medellín

PACIFIC OCEAN

Cauca

Magdalena

Bogotá

COLOMBIA

Guaviare

Cali

ANDES

Equator

Caquetá

ECUADOR

BRAZIL

Putumayo

PERU   Amazon

N

0   100   200 miles
0   160   320 kilometers

COLOMBIA'S BEGINNINGS

Colombia is part of the South American continent. The western half of the country has tall mountain ranges, deep valleys, and high plains. The eastern half is mostly low-lying jungle.

Early History

Before the 1500s, Colombia was home to a variety of Native American **tribes**. In other parts of the continent, tribes such as the Aztecs and the Incas had created sophisticated **civilizations**. But there was nothing of that kind in Colombia. Most people lived simple lives, through hunting and farming.

HOT SPOT BRIEFING

NEW GRANADA
The original Spanish name for the land that is now Colombia was New Granada. In 1549, Bogotá became its capital city.

Native Americans in Colombia left behind cave paintings like this one. These deer-like animals were probably hunted by prehistoric tribes.

Spanish Invasion

Spanish forces invaded Colombia in the early 1500s. They met with little opposition, and by the middle of the 1500s they had complete control. The Spanish brought European diseases, such as smallpox, with them. The original peoples of Colombia had no protection against these diseases, and died in great numbers.

An Unequal Society

Under the Spanish, Colombia was an unequal society. At the top were a few wealthy Spaniards. At the bottom were hundreds of thousands of slaves. The surviving Native Americans were forced to work for the Spanish in mines or in the fields. Later, slaves would be brought over from Africa to work for Spanish landowners.

The word Colombia comes from the name of Christopher Columbus (center), who led the first Europeans to the South American mainland in 1498.

SPANISH RULE

Spain ruled what is now Colombia from the early 1500s to 1819. From the beginning, the Spanish stamped out the local Native American culture and brought in their own customs, language and the Roman Catholic religion.

Spanish Aims

Spain aimed to make money from Colombia. At first, the Spanish were mostly interested in finding gold and other precious metals. They did find these in Colombia, but not in great quantities. Next, the Spanish concentrated on farming. Colombia's land was divided up between the conquerors, and made into vast farms. Their owners became increasingly rich and powerful. Their workers remained poor and powerless.

HOT SPOT BRIEFING

EL DORADO
In the early years of their rule, the Spanish heard rumors of a place where gold was plentiful. It was called El Dorado. They searched and searched, but eventually had to accept that El Dorado did not exist.

Cartagena was Colombia's main port during the Spanish era. This ancient walled city is now a World Heritage Site.

Seeking Independence

By the end of the 1700s, Colombia's wealthy elite had grown tired of being ruled by Spain. They wanted to run their own affairs and stop paying taxes to the Spanish government. They also wanted keep all the profits from their production and trade. A war broke out between Spain and its Colombian **colony**. Colombia won, and in 1819 it became an independent **state** called the Federation of Gran Colombia.

HOT SPOT BRIEFING

FEDERATION OF GRAN COLOMBIA
In addition to present-day Colombia, in 1819 the Federation of Gran Colombia included present-day Venezuela, Ecuador, and Panama and parts of surrounding countries. Venezuela and Ecuador split away in 1830, and Panama in 1903.

Between 1819 and 1830, the Federation of Gran Colombia covered modern-day Colombia, Venezuela, Ecuador, and Panama, along with small parts of Peru, Brazil, and Guyana.

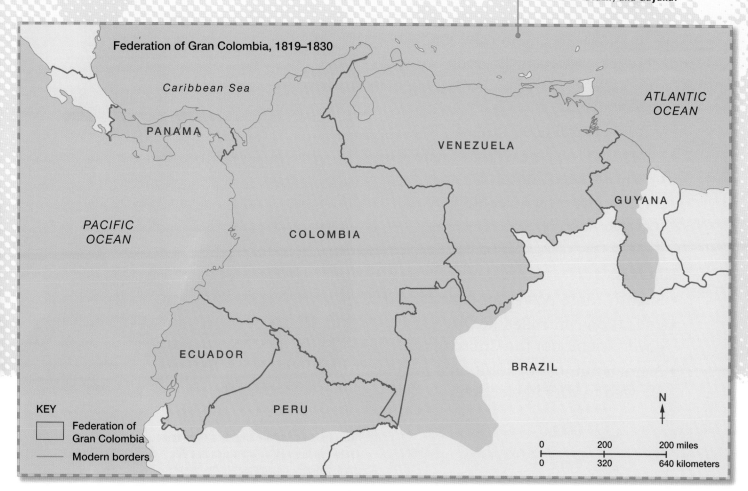

Federation of Gran Colombia, 1819–1830

Caribbean Sea

PANAMA

ATLANTIC OCEAN

VENEZUELA

PACIFIC OCEAN

GUYANA

COLOMBIA

ECUADOR

BRAZIL

PERU

KEY

☐ Federation of Gran Colombia

— Modern borders

N

| 0 | 200 | 200 miles |
| 0 | 320 | 640 kilometers |

1900s: MODERNIZATION

In the early 1900s, Colombian society began to change. Profits from the coffee trade were used to set up modern industries in the cities. Many people moved from the countryside to the towns to work in the new factories and businesses.

Two Parties

Since independence, Colombia's government had switched between two political parties, the Conservatives and the Liberals. There were slight differences between the two:

Conservatives:

- Strong central government
- Education to be heavily influenced by the Roman Catholic Church
- Strict limits on who could vote in elections

Liberals:

- Slightly more power for regions
- Education controlled by the government, not the Church
- A small number of additional people allowed to vote in elections

Workers manufacture steel in a Colombian factory in the 1940s. Industries like this attracted poor Colombians to the towns.

Interests in Common

The differences between Colombia's Conservative and Liberal parties were less important than the things they had in common. Both parties represented the interests of the wealthy elite. Both parties would do almost anything to make sure the rich stayed rich, whatever the cost to poor Colombians.

A VIOLENT COUNTRY

Between 1819 and 1902, Colombia experienced:
- eight national civil wars
- fourteen local civil wars
- two wars with neighboring Ecuador

The Colombian elite enjoyed their own luxuries. In this 1947 photo, wealthy guests relax around the pool at Bogotá's Nutibara Hotel.

CIVIL WAR: *LA VIOLENCIA*

Between 1948 and 1953, Colombia was gripped by a terrible civil war. It was named *La Violencia* (The Violence). On one side were people who wanted life for poor Colombians to improve. On the other side were those who wanted to keep their wealth and privileges as before.

Jorge Gaitán

In 1947, Jorge Gaitán took over as leader of the Liberal Party. He promised a better deal for the poor, with improvements in health, education, and land ownership for poorer Colombians. Most of the wealthy elite, including most Liberals, opposed these **reforms**. On April 9, 1948, Gaitán was shot dead in Colombia's capital, Bogotá.

> "The people [came] pouring out ... streaming down from the hills ... a hurricane of pain and anger flooding the city, smashing store windows, overturning streetcars, setting buildings afire."
>
> Latin American historian Eduardo Galeano describing the aftermath of Jorge Gaitán's murder.

Crowds gather in Bogotá for a memorial rally following the 1947 murder of Jorge Gaitán.

The Spread of Violence

After Gaitán's murder, fighting broke out in Bogotá. People who supported Gaitán's vision of change clashed with those who wanted things to stay as they were. Many people died, and property was ruined. Soon the whole country was plunged into civil war. The new Conservative government targeted anyone who argued for change, and Gaitán's followers fought back. More than 200,000 people were killed, many with extreme cruelty.

Army Rule

In 1953, an army general, Gustavo Rojas Pinilla, took power. He was allowed to do so by the Conservatives and Liberals, who hoped that Rojas could end the violence. He succeeded in doing this, but only temporarily. The wealthy elite blocked his attempts to introduce reforms to help poor Colombians. In 1957, the old political parties removed General Rojas from government.

"I'm just a *campesino* [poor farmer]
I didn't start the fight
But if they come asking for trouble
They'll get what's coming to them."

Popular song from the years of *La Violencia*.

Residents and police inspect the remains of houses, destroyed by fire and explosives in the town of Arauca during *La Violencia*.

ELECTIONS AND THE NATIONAL FRONT

In 1956, all Colombians got the right to vote in elections. This was a serious threat to the rule of the Conservative and Liberal parties. Poor Colombians would now be able to vote them out of power. In response, in 1957, a National Front government was announced.

Government Agreement

The National Front government would last until 1974, with no new elections needed until then. The Conservative and Liberal parties would take turns in government, starting with the Liberals and changing every four years. The two parties agreed to share out government jobs and to consult each other regularly.

Government in Practice

The National Front agreement ended the rivalry between the Conservatives and Liberals and their wealthy supporters. But it did nothing to stop the conflict between the elite and the rest of the people. The National Front governments allowed the elite to follow their own interests. They resisted other Colombians' calls for more land and improvements in **social welfare**.

Members of the ruling Liberal Party, led by President Alberto Lleras Camargo (center, front row) march through the streets of Bogotá in 1959.

Falling Apart

During the National Front years, Colombian society began to fall apart. Poor Colombians saw that the government made laws to benefit the rich. The police and army used violence to make sure the laws were obeyed. Meanwhile, the poor still had no land. They lived in small, uncomfortable homes, with hardly any money for food or clothes. Most people saw little point in obeying a government that treated its people so unfairly.

In 1968, children from one of Bogotá's poorer districts collect water for drinking, washing, and cooking. Families like these did not have running water at home.

HOT SPOT BRIEFING

COLOMBIA AND COFFEE
Colombia's economy depended on the price of coffee, because coffee accounted for more than half of the country's exports. In 1957, there was a sudden drop in the world price of coffee. Colombia's economy was badly affected and took almost ten years to recover.

LAND OWNERSHIP

STATISTICS

In Colombia during the last quarter of the 1900s:
- Three percent of farmers owned more than 70 percent of the agricultural land.
- Another 40 percent of farmers owned 27 percent of the agricultural land.
- The remaining 57 percent had to survive on less than 3 percent of the agricultural land.

GUERRILLAS

In the 1960s, **guerrilla** groups began to appear in Colombia. They aimed to fight against the country's wealthy elite, whose members had kept all the power and money to themselves for more than a hundred years.

Unchanging Society

Colombia's wealth grew in the late 1960s and early 1970s, but this wealth was not shared. Most Colombians, both in the cities and in the countryside, still lived in poverty. They had no legal way of pressing for change because both political parties represented the wealthy elite. Instead, some began to use violence.

The leader of the ELN (on the left) and a fellow guerrilla talk to a priest in February 1970, in the north-eastern Colombian mountains.

HOT SPOT BRIEFING

GUERRILLA GROUPS
Colombia's three main guerrilla groups were:
- FARC (*Fuerzas Armadas Revolucionarias de Colombia*: Revolutionary Armed Forces of Colombia)
- ELN (*Ejército de Liberación Nacional*: National Liberation Army)
- M-19 (*Movimiento 19 de Abril*: 19th of April Movement)

Guerrilla Groups

Two armed guerrilla groups, the FARC and ELN, were formed in 1964. Both were **left-wing** groups, fighting in the countryside. Their first aim was to defend the poor against government violence. Their second was to overthrow the wealthy elite and create a more equal society. In 1974, a third group, M-19, was formed. M-19's aims were the same as FARC and ELN's, but it was based in the cities.

Successes

Colombia's three guerrilla groups gained some strong victories in their wars against the Colombian army and police. FARC and ELN managed to take over large areas of the countryside. However, they never became powerful enough to overthrow the government.

An injured man is carried from Bogotá's Palace of Justice, during its seizure by M-19 guerrillas in 1985. More than one hundred people were killed when the army stormed the building on the following day.

THE DRUG TRADE

Around the end of the 1960s, a new problem arose in Colombia—the drug trade. Colombian farmers began growing marijuana, which had become very popular in North America. Then, in the mid-1970s, they switched to producing another illegal drug: cocaine.

A Colombian farmer checks the progress of his coca crop in the southern jungle province of Putumayo.

Buyers and Sellers

Colombians recognized that they could make a lot of money by selling drugs abroad. Buyers in North America and Europe would import the drugs in great quantities, even though it was against the law. Cocaine was made from the coca plant, which was cheap and easy for farmers to grow. Peru and Bolivia grew coca too, but Colombia soon became the center of the cocaine trade. The Colombian **drug barons** who ran the trade became extremely rich.

HOT SPOT BRIEFING

COCAINE USE
Cocaine has been illegal in most countries since the early 1900s, but is still used by more than 13 million people around the world.

Cocaine and Conflict

The cocaine trade caused conflict throughout Colombia. The drug barons fought among themselves, sparking waves of criminal violence. They used their wealth to **bribe** politicians and judges, which weakened people's trust in the country's legal system. The guerrillas supported poor farmers in their decision to grow coca, because it helped them to earn money. The guerrillas started selling drugs to pay for their own activities.

In a hidden jungle laboratory, a man begins the process of turning coca leaves into cocaine.

COLOMBIA AND THE UNITED STATES

Governments in the United States have always kept watch on Latin America. Throughout the **Cold War** (1947–1989), the United States wanted to stop **communists** from gaining support in the area. From the 1960s onwards, the drug problem also became a major concern.

The War on Drugs

The use of illegal drugs in the United States increased at an alarming rate through the 1960s and 1970s. U.S. governments were unable to stop many of their citizens from wanting these drugs. Instead, the United States tried to stop drug production and transportation. Colombia was the world's biggest producer and shipper of the drug cocaine. It became one of the United States's main targets in the war on drugs.

HOT SPOT BRIEFING

SHIPPING COCAINE
During the 1970s and 1980s, most drugs from Colombia were shipped across the Caribbean in small planes and boats. In recent years, more and more shipments to the United States have gone via Mexico.

Mexican police inspect suitcases packed with cocaine, intercepted on their way from Colombia to the United States.

Supporting the Elite

The United States worked with the Colombian government to try to prevent the cocaine trade. However, by supporting the Colombian government, the United States was also helping the elite to stay in power. The gap between rich and poor Colombians stayed as it was. This increased support among the poor for the guerrillas. It also encouraged poor farmers to grow the only crop that offered them a decent living—coca.

In 1982, people in Bogotá protest against U.S. policy in Latin America. Many Colombians felt that their needs were being neglected while the United States assisted their government.

THE RISE OF THE ARMY

By the early 1980s, the Colombian government was no longer the only source of power in the country. The guerrillas controlled large areas of the countryside. The drug barons used bribes and violence to carry on their illegal trade without government interference.

Fighting for Control

The government was desperate to keep control of Colombia. It became more dependent on the army for support. The army tried to wage war on the guerrillas, but found it impossible to win a clear victory. Eventually, the army sought help from the powerful drug barons. Together, the army and drug barons organized violent **paramilitary death squads**.

"[The paramilitary groups are the] real **terrorist** organizations... The majority of their victims aren't guerrillas. They are men, women and children who have not taken up arms ... [who] are peaceful Colombians."

Colombia's President Barco, speaking in 1989.

Masked members of a paramilitary death squad patrol near the town of Doradal, on the road to the drug center of Medellín.

Death Squads

The death squads were unable to catch the guerrillas. Instead, they began to torture or kill anyone suspected of helping the rebels. The death squads murdered thousands of innocent people. Many poor Colombians felt they had no choice but to ask the guerrillas to protect them.

MURDER CAPITAL

In 1996, there were 9,500 murders in the Colombian city of Medellín, one of the centers of the drug trade. New York City, with a population five times larger, had less than 400 murders that year.

Child refugees who have escaped the violence between death squads and guerrillas are given food in a Bogotá camp.

A FAILING STATE

By the end of the 1980s, Colombia was in danger of becoming a country without effective government—a failed state. Violence affected everyone, including politicians who spoke out against the drug barons. In 1990, three candidates in the presidential elections were murdered.

War on the Drug Barons

In the early 1990s, Colombia's government finally declared war on the drug barons. The most famous, Pablo Escobar, was killed by the police in 1993. Escobar's criminal organization, the Medellín Cartel, was no longer the most powerful in the cocaine trade. Unfortunately for the government, another organization, the Cali Cartel, took the Medellín Cartel's place.

HOT SPOT BRIEFING

GARBAGE
In the 1990s, the economy was so bad that it was estimated that 30,000 Colombians lived off other people's rubbish, by collecting it and selling it for recycling.

Army soldiers raid the home of Pablo Escobar, chief of the Medellín drug cartel and Colombia's most wanted man. Soon afterward, Escobar was caught and killed.

A Bleak Future?

By the 1990s, many Colombians had lost all hope of a better future. Their politicians were powerless, **corrupt** or both. The guerrillas, who had started out fighting for the poor, now appeared to be more interested in fighting each other. They were selling drugs and **kidnapping** well-known people for **ransom**. The future seemed bleak.

"Your actions have ... turned Colombia into a battleground... Your war lost its political validity [its point] some time ago."

From an open letter to the guerrillas, sent by 50 Colombian artists, journalists and academics in 1992.

Relations and friends of missing and kidnapped persons demand the return of their loved ones in Medellín, June 2000.

PLAN COLOMBIA

In 1999, President Pastrana launched a project called Plan Colombia. He hoped his proposals would rescue the country from violence and improve life for Colombian people.

The Plan's Aims

Plan Colombia aimed for:

- peace talks with the guerrillas
- greater efforts to stop the drug trade
- a revival of the economy
- a strengthening of **democracy**
- greater respect for **human rights**

Paying for the Plan

The government could not pay for Plan Colombia on its own. The United States provided money for the wars against the guerrillas and the drug trade, but not for anything else. The **European Union** offered little help.

Plan Colombia was unpopular with the guerrillas. Here, a member of FARC stands in front of a poster picturing Plan Colombia as a U.S. boot holding Colombia down.

Talks with the Guerrillas

As part of Plan Colombia, the government tried to negotiate with the guerrillas. A series of meetings took place with FARC and ELN in 1998 through 2000, but no agreement was reached. The guerrillas refused to give up their weapons. They feared that unless the death squads were also **disarmed**, many former guerrillas would quickly be killed.

The Drug War Goes On

Through the 2000s, the war against the drug trade went on. The Colombian army succeeded in destroying many jungle laboratories. The air force, with U.S. help, sprayed large areas with toxic chemicals to destroy the coca plantations. But despite all these efforts, the amount of cocaine produced in Colombia continued to increase.

COCA GROWTH

STATISTICS

Coca production in Colombia increased by 15 percent between 2000 and 2006. This was despite the efforts of the Colombian army, and U.S. aid of more than $5 billion in its war against drugs.

Army troops perform anti-drug duties in the Colombian jungle. Behind the rising helicopter, a cocaine laboratory has been set on fire.

COLOMBIA IN THE 2000s

In 2002, Alvaro Uribe was elected president. He set out to defeat the guerrillas and the drug barons. President Uribe cut health and education spending, and used the money to double the size of the army.

Uribe's Failure

Uribe's efforts failed. The territory controlled by the guerrillas shrank, but they were not defeated. Attempts to stop the drug trade were even less successful. This was partly because the Colombian government could not do anything about the North Americans and Europeans who bought cocaine, and made the trade possible. But Uribe also failed to offer poor Colombian coca farmers other ways of earning a living.

> "All along I knew we weren't making any progress. But I was just a field commander. The big shots in Washington just told me to shut up."
>
> Terry Nelson, who spent 32 years fighting drugs as a U.S. government representative in Latin America.

President Alvaro Uribe makes a speech as he takes office in August 2002.

Colombia's Future

It seems that Colombia's problems will be difficult to solve if society remains so unequal in the future. But if the poor were able to improve their lives, the guerrillas would have less support in their fight against the government. If the poor were treated more fairly, they would have reason to respect the law and the people who enforce it. This would make life much harder for the drug dealers.

"Of course we need to eliminate social injustice in Colombia, but what is first? Peace. Without peace, there is no investment. Without investment, there [is no money] to invest in the welfare of the people."

President Uribe, November 18, 2004.

Demonstrators light candles during a 90-hour-long protest against FARC in Bogotá in February 2009. Messages of support were sent by radio and the Internet to hostages being held by FARC.

FACTFINDER: Colombia

Full name Republic of Colombia

Capital Bogotá

Area 439,736 square miles
(1,138,910 square kilometers)

Population 45,644,023 (July 2009 estimate)

Rate of population change +1.38% per year

Religions Roman Catholic 90%
Other 10%

Industries (legal, non-drug) Textiles, food processing, oil, clothing, and footwear

Gross Domestic Product* per person US$8,900

Percentage of labor force in agriculture 22.4%

Percentage of labor force in industry 18.8%

Percentage of labor force in services 58.8%

Number of phone lines 7.936 million (in 2007)

Number of TV stations 60 (in 2009)

> * Gross Domestic Product, or GDP, is the value of all the goods and services produced by a country in a year.
> (Source for statistics: *CIA World Factbook*)

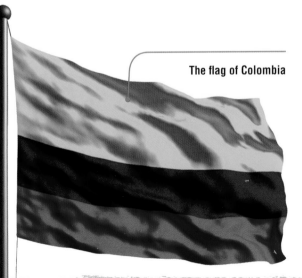

The flag of Colombia

FOCUS QUESTIONS

These questions might help you to think about some of the issues raised in *Colombia*.

Leadership and Government

What different systems of government has Colombia had since it was founded?
During the National Front years, was Colombia a democracy?

Economy

What is Colombia's most valuable industry?
Is the money from Colombian industries and agriculture shared out fairly?

Politics

Which other countries have tried to help Colombians improve their lives?
Have the actions of other countries made life better or worse for Colombian people?

Citizenship

Do most Colombians support the government?
Why do some Colombians support the guerrillas?
Who benefits from the cocaine trade, and who is harmed by it?

GLOSSARY

bribe money paid to gain unfair influence over decisions

cartel group of businesses working together, often used to describe drug gangs

civilization society that has developed its own culture

civil war war between different groups within their own country

cocaine illegal drug made from the leaves of the coca plant

Cold War decades of hostility (1947–1989) between the U.S.-led capitalist world and the Soviet-led communist world

colony country ruled by another country

communist based on a system where the government, rather than individual people, owns and runs farms, factories, and businesses

corrupt giving or taking money in exchange for doing something illegal

culture things that make a society or people distinctive, such as their language, clothes, food, music, songs, and stories

death squad unofficial group formed to murder political opponents

democracy political system that allows people to vote for their government

disarm remove weapons

drug barons leaders of criminal gangs involved in the drug trade

elite small group of people at the top of society, usually the richest and most powerful

European Union group of European countries that work closely together

guerrilla hit-and-run fighter, often one who aims to overthrow a government

hostage prisoner held and used as exchange for money or political advantage

human rights basic rights such as freedom of speech

kidnapping illegally taking and holding someone prisoner

left-wing politically tending to place the needs of the community above those of the individual

marijuana plant and illegal drug

paramilitary organized like a military force, but not part of the official army

ransom money paid in return for freeing a hostage

reforms social or political changes

social welfare help given to people who are unable to support themselves

state area under a single government

terrorist someone who carries out violence to scare others

tribe group of people with a common language and traditions

INDEX